Self-publish your book using CreateSpace: an Amazon print-on-demand service

MARY HOWARD

Copyright © 2017 by Mary Howard

All rights reserved.

Author's Profile: www.amazon.com/author/maryhoward

Email author: maryhowardpublications@gmail.com

ISBN-13: 978-1514889725

ISBN-10: 1514889722

Published by Howard Designs & Publications.

Printed by CreateSpace.

Cover image is from Cover Creator Image Library at CreateSpace.

This book is for sale at Amazon.

CONTENTS

Planning your book project, 3

Overview of CreateSpace homepage, 5

Signing up for a free CreateSpace, 6

Copying and pasting the Service Agreement, 7

Verifying your email address, 8

Setting up your first book, 9

Entering the title information and getting your free ISBN, 10

Making a cover for your book, 11

Downloading a template for your book, 12

Putting your book's document into the template, 13

Converting the template document into a PDF document, 15

Uploading the book's Interior PDF file, 16

Proofing your book, 18

Estimating the cost to buy copies of your book, 19

Buying copies of your book, 20

Making your book available for sale on Amazon, 21

Appendix A: How to create an invisible table with an image and text description, 22

Appendix B: How to save Clipart as a .jpg file to use in your book, 23

Appendix C: How to use a scanned image in your book, 24

INTRODUCTION

The instructions in this workbook are the same ones that were used to make the book itself.

You will learn how to make a book of any size, as few as 10 pages, or as many as 600. It can be done in black and white or in full color. You can use your real name as the author or choose a pen-name. When you are done, you can order one copy of your book or hundreds. The options are many.

Although the focus of this workbook is on publishing a book for personal or business reasons, there are a few instructions on how to make your book available for sale on distribution channels, such as Amazon.com, if you think others would enjoy reading it too.

Publishing your first book will be one of the most rewarding ventures you will ever do. And once you find out how easy it is, you can make many books.

So let's get started!

Planning your book project

The first thing you should do is create three folders to save files, links, and emails that relate to your book project.

A – In your email account, create a new folder called "My Book Project" or use the title of your book as the name. Any emails you get from CreateSpace or any others relating to your book project, move them into this folder.

B – In your Favorites List in Internet Explorer, create a new folder called "My Book Project" or use the title of your book as the name. Save any webpages that relate to your project in this folder. For example, if you sell your book on Amazon.com you will have a URL that goes to your book sales page.

C – In your Documents directory on your PC, create a new folder called "My Book Project" or use the title of your book as the name. As an alternative, you can buy a flash-drive and save all your files relating to your book project on it. This is a more secure method since files on a flash-drive are not affected in the event of computer failure. Create sub-folders (like Interior Files) to keep things organized.

On a pad of paper, write down the following information about your book. Use it when you are setting up your book title information.

   a) The title of your book
   b) The sub-title (if one)
   c) Author(s)
   d) A description of your book
   e) Approximate number of pages
   f) The trim size you want (6"x9" is recommended for trade paperbacks)
   g) Whether the interior of the book will be in black-and-white or full-colour.

h) What image you would like to use for the front cover.
i) A brief back-cover outline.

The instructions below are done in segments so that you aren't doing everything all at once. If you work on your project a little each day it will take about a week to complete.

I recommended scanning through the entire workbook before you actually begin to do your first book project. This will give you a general idea of what you will be doing.

Overview of CreateSpace homepage

1. Go to **www.createspace.com**
2. On the left side is the login section. On the right side are links to information, tools, and success stories.
3. Scroll down to the section called "Independent Publishing with CreateSpace".
4. Here you will see links to some very useful information pages. You can read some of these at your leisure.

Signing up for a free CreateSpace account

The basic services at CreateSpace are free. However they do offer some paid services that you can use. The instructions in this book are geared towards the free services.

1. Go to **www.createspace.com**
2. In the top-right corner, click "Sign Up".
3. Fill out the following areas: a) email address b) password (and re-enter) c) first name d) last name e) choose your country f) choose the type of media you are considering publishing (in this case *Book*)
4. Leave the box for fee-based services blank. You can look into it later.
5. Click "Create My Account".

Copying and pasting the Service Agreement

You will come to the **CreateSpace Service Agreement**. This is an important document that you should read. I recommend copying it and pasting it into a Word document and saving it so that you can refer to it whenever you need to.

1. Highlight and hold the mouse button as you scroll down the entire document.
2. Press Ctrl-C on your computer.
3. Open a new blank document in Word 2010.
4. Press Ctrl-V to paste the agreement into the blank document.
5. Save the file in your My Book Project folder. Save as a Word document or a PDF document. Later, in your spare time, review this agreement, especially if you plan to sell your book through Amazon.com.
6. Now back on your webpage screen, select "I agree to all terms" at the bottom of the agreement.
7. Click "Continue".

Verifying your email address

1. Open your email account.
2. Look in your Inbox for the email from CreateSpace.
3. Click the blue link to verify your email address.
4. You will come to a Login screen.
5. Login into your account using your email address and password.

Setting up your first book

1. Click "Set up your book now".
2. Type in the title of your book.
3. Select "Paperback".
4. Select *getting started* for "Guided: a step-by-step process with help along the way".
5. For now, click the "Member Dashboard" on the left side of the screen.
6. Click the link of your book title.
7. You will come to a section that shows each step you will be making to finish your project. In the "Setup and Review" section, all the steps are required to publish your book. The section for "Distribution, Sales, and Marketing" are optional for people who want to make their book available for sale.

First, let me give you an overview of this page.

1. Notice the list of steps you will make to complete your book. a) Title Information b) ISBN c) Interior d) Cover e) Complete Setup.
2. In the top-left corner is the link to your "Member Dashboard". This is the screen you will always come to when your first log in to your account.
3. If you want help from the Support Staff of CreateSpace, click "Contact Support" on the left side.
4. At the bottom of the page are helpful tips and ideas for creating a book.
5. In the top-right corner is your Logout link.

Entering the title information and getting your free ISBN

1. Click the book link in the "My Projects" section of your Member Dashboard.
2. In the "Setup" section, select "Title Information".
3. You will notice that the only two required fields are the "title" and the "primary author". If you are making a private book for yourself, family or friends, this is all you will need to enter. But if you are planning to make the book available for sale, then it is important to have a complete "description" of your book.
4. When you are done, click "Save & Continue" at the bottom.
5. Choose the first option "Free CreateSpace-Assigned ISBN". This is the best option because you can sell your book anywhere, including through schools and libraries, as well as on Amazon sites.
6. Click "Assign Free ISBN".
7. Now write both ISBN numbers on a piece of paper. You are going to need to put them on the copyright page of your book's Interior file later.
8. Now logout out of your CreateSpace account.

Making a cover for your book

1. Login to your CS account.
2. Click the book title link.
3. In the "Setup" section, click "Cover".
4. Choose "Build Your Cover Online".
5. Click "Launch Cover Creator".
6. You will come to a section with an array of template designs. Choose one you like. For example, I choose the "Hawthorne 6x9 Spineless" theme on page 3 for this workbook.
7. On the left side are tasks that you can complete. Not all of them are mandatory. Go through each one and make your selection. Enter the required information. Click "Next" to go to the next task.
8. When you get to the "Image" task, you can either choose one of the free images provided or you can upload an image from your computer. (see the Appendix section for some ideas)
9. Be sure to type an interesting "Back Cover Text". NOTE: The more text you enter, the smaller the print will be on the back cover.
10. When you are satisfied, click "Submit Cover" at the bottom-right corner.
11. Click the center link that says "Full-Size Preview" to see what your cover will look like. Close window.
12. If you are pleased, click "Complete Cover". If not, click "Edit Cover" and make your changes.
13. When you are done, logout.

TIP: In my personal experience, I found the "Oak" template to be the best one to use. It has all the criteria and it looks good once you have your background colors entered. Also, it is better to use an image from CreateSpace's Image Library because they have the correct DPI for the image. When you are beginning as a self-publisher, it's not a bad place to start.

Downloading a template for your book

When you use a template for your book, the title and author's name will be on the top of each page respectively, and the margins will be aligned correctly.

1. Visit:

   https://www.createspace.com/en/community/docs/DOC-1323

   Look for the size you want your book to be in the left column. The 6"x9" trim size is recommended for both fiction and non-fiction.
2. The instructions in this book are for formatted templates because you will get the best quality book.
3. Click the "Download" blue link. Choose "Save As". Save the file in your book project folder.

Putting your book's document into the template

1. Open Word 2010.
2. Click File. Click Open.
3. Select the file "CreateSpace Formatted Template" in your book project folder. Click "Open".
4. Re-save the file using the book title as your file name and enter the number 1. Example: *Bob's Barbecue Recipes 1*. Each time you work on the book, save the file under another number. Then all your changes will safeguarded in case you change your mind.
5. Scroll down the document and replace the text as appropriate. Start with the "Book Title" then put your name in the "Author" area. Choose a prominent font for this area that is different from the text font of your book.
6. On the next page, fill in your copyright ownership. This can be your name or a company name.
7. Enter the ISBNs on the copyright page. These will be checked by the CreateSpace team when your book is submitted for review.
8. The next sections are: Dedication, Contents, and Acknowledgements. This are optional. If you don't want these, simply delete the page and the following blank one.
9. Now you will come to Chapter 1 section. I recommend only inserting headers for novels or non-fiction with definite chapters. Position the cursor on the page with the header "Author". Now click "Insert" on the menu bar. Select "Header". At the bottom of this dialog box, click "Edit Header". Replace the text with your name in all caps. Click the red x box "Close Header" on the menu bar. Do the same thing with the "Book Title". Check to make sure your Author name is on the even page numbers and the Book Title is on the odd page numbers. NOTE: you can also

change the font of the headers by simply highlighting it, selecting Home, and then choosing the font you are going to do the book in.
10. Now you can replace the template text for your chapters with your book text. You can also insert .jpg images, clip art, photos, anywhere in the document. Any pages that you don't use in the template, simply delete. TIP: It is easier to type your notes in a draft Word document first and then copy and paste the notes into your template. Remember to adjust your fonts and your line-spacing, so everything is neat and tidy.
11. When you are done, click "Save As" and put in the next number for your file name. Example: *Bob's Barbecue Recipes 2.*

Converting the template document into a **PDF** document

Once you have finished your book in the Word document, and have edited it to your satisfaction, you can then save it as a PDF.

1. Open the Word document for your book.
2. Click "File". Click "Save As".
3. Under "Save as type" at the bottom section of the dialog box, choose "PDF".
4. In the "File Name" section, type the book title with a line between each word. For example: *Bob's_Barbecue_Recipes*
5. Click "Save".
6. The document will then open in Acrobat Reader. You can scroll down to make sure everything looks OK.

Uploading the book's Interior PDF file

1. Login to your CS account.
2. Click the book title link.
3. In the "Setup" section, choose "Interior".
4. Make your selections in the Interior Type. For my own experience, I found the "cream" to be more of a light-yellow in color. It is suitable more for a novel than non-fiction. The 6"x9" trim size is ideal for both fiction and non-fiction.
5. Below, choose "Upload your Book File".
6. Now click "Browse". Locate your book project folder. Highlight the PDF file of your book. Click "Open".
7. Select the "Bleed" for your book. For this workbook, I used the second one "Ends before the edge of the book".
8. Make sure the box is checked for "Run automated print checks and view formatting issues online".
9. Click "Save".
10. Wait for your file to be processed in the "Automated Print Check". It will take a few minutes. NOTE: You will receive an email from CreateSpace explaining any issues that result from the automated print check.
11. When it is done, click "Launch Interior Reviewer" to see any issues with your file.
12. On the right side the issues will be shown. NOTE: Font issues will be automatically corrected when you submit your project. Also, images don't have to be perfect to look acceptable in the final book.
13. Click "Get Started".
14. Click on the arrow button next to the Title page of your book. Go through each page to make sure everything looks OK.
15. If you are satisfied, click "Save and Continue". If not, click "Go back and Make changes".

16. When everything looks fine to you, click "Ignore Issues and Continue". If not, click "Upload a different file" and repeat the process above until you are satisfied.
17. Click the button "Return to Project Home" in the top-left area of the screen.
18. You will notice that all the items in the Setup section are checked off in green, except "Complete Setup". If any of these items are not checked, click the button to read the message telling you what action to take.
19. Now, select "Complete Setup".
20. Review each item to make sure everything is accurate. Read the information about the Review Process.
21. When everything is OK, click "Submit Files For Review".
22. Logout of your account.
23.

NOTE: It will take a couple of days for the review to take place. The support staff of CreateSpace will send you an email and let you know if there are any changes to be made. If none are needed, they will tell you when to do your proof.

Proofing your book

1. Login to your CS account.
2. Click the book title link.
3. Under the "Review" section, select "Proof Your Book".
4. The easiest way to proof-read it is to use the online digital proofer provided. You can also order a copy by mail and proof it manually.
5. When you are satisfied, click "Approve".

Estimating the cost to buy copies of your book

You can do this calculation at any time, even before you sign up for an account with CreateSpace. This section is for your information only.

1. Go to **www.createspace.com**
2. Scroll down to "Independent Publishing with CreateSpace".
3. Click the "economics" link in the "Higher Royalties" section.
4. Part way down, click "Buying Copies".
5. Review this page. Make your calculations to get the unit price, plus shipping cost, for your book. Notice that it is cheaper to order 10 or more copies than a single book.

EXAMPLE

Full Colour Interior

Trim Size: 8x10

Number of pages: 25

Quantity: 10

Price: $3.65 each

Shipping Calculation:

Standard Shipping to Canada (9 business days) $20.99

Priority Shipping to Canada (2 business days) $35.99

In reality, it took one week for me to get my books shipped to my B.C. address using Priority Shipping.

You will need a real address (and not a post-box) to get your books shipped to you by Priority Shipping. Otherwise, you must choose Standard Shipping.

Buying copies of your book

1. Login to your CS account.
2. On the right side of your book title link, choose the link that says "Order Copies".
3. Complete the Shopping Cart information to process your purchase.
4. Save or print the receipt. You will also get a copy sent to your email account. You will be notified by email when your books are shipped.
5. Logout of your CS account.

Making your book available for sale on Amazon

1. Login to your CS account.
2. Click the book title link.
3. Under the "Distribute" section, choose "Channels".
4. Select each channel you want to distribute your book through.
5. Click "Save & Continue".
6. Now enter the list price of your book.
7. Click "Calculate". On the right side, the royalty amounts will show for each channel.
8. When you are satisfied, click "Save & Continue".
9. Now complete the detailed description section. Include any information you want prospective buyers to know.
10. Click "Save & Continue".
11. You are now finished.
12. Logout of your CS account.

Appendix A - How to create an invisible table with an image and text description

1. Open Word 2010.
2. Click "Insert".
3. Click "Table".
4. Select "Insert Table".
5. Enter 1 for the number of columns and 2 for the number of rows.
6. Position the cursor in the first row and select "Center" on the Home menu.
7. Click "Insert". Select "Picture" or "Clipart". Choose the image you want and insert it in the top box of the table. You can adjust the size of the image by right-clicking the cursor and following the instructions.
8. Now position the cursor in the bottom box of the table. Type your description of the image.
9. Make any adjustments or corrections.
10. When you are finished, click "Page Layout" on the menu bar.
11. Select "Page Borders". Click the "Borders" tab.
12. In the Preview section on the right side, click each bar line to make the borders disappear. Select OK.
13. Notice how the color of the table lines change. This means that when the table is printed, the lines of the table will not show.
14. To see what the table will look like in your finished book, select "File" and then "Print". On the right side you will see what the printed page will look like. Click "View" to return to your document.
15. Save the table.

NOTE: This type of table is ideal for doing a memoirs book. You can put the photo on the top section and a description of it on the bottom section.

Appendix B – How to save Clipart as a .jpg file to use in your book

1. Open Word 2010.
2. In a blank document, click "Insert", select "Clipart".
3. On the right side, type in a keyword or phrase that describes what image you want to see. Click the "Go" button. Example: **barbecue**
4. Now browse down the list and choose one you would like to put in your book.
5. Highlight the image and right-click your mouse. Click "Save picture as".
6. Open your book project folder.
7. Save the image using a name you will remember. Save as type "JPEG".
8. Later, insert this image in your book document. You can also upload an image to your book cover.

CHANGE COLOR

This is a useful tool for changing a color image to black-and-white.

1. Right-click the image. Choose "Format Picture".
2. Select "Picture Color".
3. Select "Presets" button under "Recolor".
4. Make your selection.
5. Click close.

You can also choose "Picture", then "Color", then choose "Black & White".

Appendix C – How to use a scanned image in your book

You will need a scanner or an all-in-one printer to make a scanned image.

This function is useful for scanning drawings, small paintings, children's artwork, sketches, and even things like old photographs.

1. Place the item you would like scanned under the lid of your printer-scanner.
2. Press the "Scan" button.
3. The scanned image will be saved in your image directory file.
4. Re-name the file to something that is easy to identify.
5. Copy this scan file into your book project folder.
6. Use the scanned image in the same way you would a photo or clipart.

Post your Review

If you have benefited from reading this book, please post a favorable review on my Amazon book page. Thank you.

Other books by the author:

Write an *amazing* bestseller!

Self-publish your book as a Kindle ebook at Amazon's KDP

Visit my author's profile page at:
www.amazon.com/author/maryhoward

Email author: maryhowardpublications@gmail.com

Printed in Great Britain
by Amazon